Awakening a Kind Heart

A Guide to the
Four Immeasurables and the
Eight Verses of Thought Transformation

Sangye Khadro

For Free Distribution

Published in 1996
Amitabha Buddhist Centre
494-D Geylang Road
Singapore 389452

 Printed entirely on Recycled Paper

Awakening a Kind Heart first published in *The Golden Link*,
Ngee Ann Polytechnic, 1991. Reprinted as *Awakening a Kind Heart:
The Practice of the Four Immeasurables*, ABC, 1994.
*Training The Mind in Compassion: An Explanation of the
Eight Verses of Thought Transformation* by Langri Tangpa
first published 1996.

ISBN 981 00 5168 9

Dedicated to
the long lives
of all
spiritual
teachers
teaching
true paths to
enlightenment,
especially
His Holiness
the Fourteenth
Dalai Lama,
a living
embodiment
of
compassion.

C*ONTENTS*

PREFACE

Whether one believes in a religion or not, and whether one believes in rebirth or not, there is no one who does not appreciate kindness and compassion.
— His Holiness the Dalai Lama[1]

Everyone appreciates kindness. A smile, a few friendly words, a show of concern when we are troubled or feeling unwell, an offer of help — gestures of kindness like these brighten our day and ease whatever sadness we may feel in our hearts. Feeling that "someone cares about me" fulfills a very deep need that we all have. And just as we appreciate other people being kind to us, others appreciate it when we are kind to them. That is why it is important to learn to be kind, because it will help make our relationships and interactions with others more satisfying and free from problems.

But it is not always easy to be kind. Sometimes our hearts are filled with anger, jealousy, or pride, and being kind is the last thing we feel like doing. Or we get so caught up in our work and responsibilities that we find no time to think of others and their needs, no time to be kind and gentle.

However, these problems can be remedied. The Buddhist tradition offers a wealth of methods that can be used to overcome whatever prevents us from being kind, such as anger or selfishness, and to bring more kindness into our daily lives.

Some of these methods are explained in this book. The first part of the book, *Awakening a Kind Heart*, is an explanation of the Four Immeasurable Thoughts — love, compassion, joy and equanimity — which are essential practices in all traditions of Buddhism. This piece is a slightly revised version of an article that I wrote in 1991 at the request of the Ngee Ann Polytechnic Buddhist Society, Singapore, for their yearly magazine, *The Golden Link*.

The second part of the book, *Training the Mind in Compassion*, is an explanation of a brief text called *The Eight Verses of Thought Transformation* composed by the eleventh-century Tibetan meditation master Geshe Langri Tangpa.[2] The *Eight Verses* is a beautiful little text, easily memorized, which offers us precious gems of wisdom on how to transform difficult situations into opportunities for spiritual growth. In other words, how to transform pain into joy and lightness. The explanation is based on a series of talks I gave at the Buddhist Library in Singapore, between November 1989 and February 1990.

This book has come about through the kindness of many people. I would first of all like to thank from the depths of my heart my teachers, especially His Holiness the Dalai Lama, Lama Thubten Yeshe, Lama Thubten Zopa Rinpoche, Geshe Ngawang Dhargyey, Geshe Jampa Tegchog, and the many other precious masters from whom I learned about kindness and compassion, not only from their teachings but from their perfect living example. I also give my heartfelt thanks to Vens Thubten Drolkar and Thubten Dechen for transcribing and typing the talks on the *Eight Verses*; to Ven Sarah Tenzin Yiwong for her input and invaluable editing of the entire manuscript;

to Doris Low, Paul Ferguson and Don Brown for their ideas and suggestions; to Ven Roger Kunsang and Jan Pether for the use of their photos; to Snow Lion Publications for permission to use the quotations of His Holiness the Dalai Lama; to Arthur Yong for designing and publishing the book; and to Koh Thong Joo for sponsoring the publication.

May this work help to bring peace and happiness to the minds and lives of all beings everywhere.

Sangye Khadro
Singapore, 1996

AWAKENING
A KIND HEART

The Practice of
The Four Immeasurables

May all sentient beings have happiness and its causes;

May all sentient beings be free of suffering and its causes;

May all sentient beings not be separated from sorrowless bliss;

May all sentient beings abide in equanimity, free of bias, attachment and anger.

INTRODUCTION:

How TO DEVELOP A KIND HEART

Do you want to be happy? Do you want to have a healthy and satisfying life? This is not an advertisement for a marvelous new health product, but an encouragement to be more kind and loving.

Everyone wants happiness and health, but not everyone realizes that loving-kindness is an essential ingredient for these. Why? Because loving-kindness frees us from self-centredness and self-importance which disturb our peace of mind. Self-centredness is the cause of such problems as hatred for enemies, envy for rivals and clinging-attachment to family and friends. These disturbing mental attitudes, if untreated, can even lead to physical ailments. Loving-kindness helps us to overcome these problems and paves the way for good relations with friend and foe alike.

A kind, loving heart values people more than things. Instead of seeking happiness solely through work, knowledge, consumer goods, sex, travel, entertainment or sports, we devote more energy to the people in our lives. We spend time with them, listening when they want to talk and sharing with them our own thoughts and feelings. In these ways our relationships grow closer and deeper. On the other hand, if we don't know how to give and receive love we won't be truly happy, no matter how many degrees we have, how wealthy we are or how high we climb on the social ladder.

You may think, "Yes, I know all that. I want to have loving-kindness, but it's so difficult." This is true. Selfishness, anger and the like arise as naturally as water flowing downhill, while being kind is as difficult as pushing a boulder uphill. But who ever said it would be easy?

Loving-kindness is difficult but not impossible. We can change ourselves. When I was young, I did not know how to get along with others. I had a bad temper, behaved selfishly, and suffered a lot because I had few friends. I wished to be like my schoolmates who were cheerful, friendly and kind, but it seemed that I was doomed to be always grumpy and unkind.

Later, I discovered Buddhism, which teaches not only that we should be kind, but *how* to be kind. The Buddha's teachings reveal a rich array of methods — such as different types of meditation, purification practices and devotional prayer — that can be used to free ourselves of negative attitudes like anger and selfishness and develop positive ones like loving-kindness and compassion. It is my experience that these methods work. Not that my anger and selfishness have completely disappeared! They still arise, but less frequently than before, and kind-heartedness arises more often.

Some people are born with an abundance of wholesome qualities. They are kind, peaceful, respectful, considerate of others and take delight in doing good deeds. They are like this because of their familiarity with these qualities in previous lives. Actually, we *all* have many good qualities, but in some of us they are less developed. That is why in Buddhism, we train ourselves to think and behave in a kind and considerate way. The more we practise being kind and helpful, the more these qualities will arise naturally and spontaneously. It's like learning to play the piano: the more you practise, the better you become.

Just as water cools
   both good and bad
And washes away
   all impurity and dust,

In the same way
   you should develop thoughts
   of love to friend
   and foe alike,
And having reached
   perfection in love,
You will attain enlightenment.
                    The Buddha

One of the best ways to develop a kind heart is through contemplating the four immeasurable thoughts: love, compassion, sympathetic joy and equanimity. They are called "immeasurable" because they extend to all beings, who are immeasurable, and because we create immeasurable positive energy and purify immeasurable negative energy through developing them. They are also called "the four sublime states" because developing them in our minds makes us like the sublime buddhas, bodhisattvas and arhats who are beyond attachment and aversion.

The four immeasurable thoughts are expressed in the following prayer:

> May all sentient beings have happiness and its causes;
> May all sentient beings be free of suffering and its causes;
> May all sentient beings not be separated from sorrowless bliss;
> May all sentient beings abide in equanimity, free of bias, attachment and anger.

By reciting this prayer slowly and sincerely one or more times each day, and reflecting on its meaning, we can develop a heart of kindness towards all beings. So let's now take a look at the meaning of each of these immeasurable thoughts.

IMMEASURABLE
L*OVE*

May all beings have happiness and its causes.

How do we come to love someone? What does it take for love to arise in our hearts? I'm not talking about the sort of love we fall into when we meet an attractive, charming or sexy person. That sort of love may not run very deep or last very long. It can disappear at the first disagreement!

The sort of love involved in immeasurable love is a genuine feeling of caring and respect for others. We wish them to be happy and to have whatever they need for a healthy, satisfying life. It can also be called loving-kindness.

Several different factors give rise to such love. One is realizing the important role people play in our lives. For example, we love our parents because they brought us into the world and give us the food, shelter, love and protection we need. They console us when we are sad or frightened and take care of us when we are sick. We love other family members and friends because we share with them the joys and sorrows of life. We love our teachers because from them we learn the knowledge and skills we need to earn a living and deal with the challenges of life.

But do we love the bus driver who takes us to work or school each day? You may think I'm joking. "I don't even know him — he's a stranger!" But remember, love is a feeling of caring and kindness. Loving someone doesn't mean we must have a close relationship. It means we care about that person, appreciate what that person does for us and wish that person happiness.

There are many people who contribute to our well-being without our realizing it. By thinking about what they do for us we can feel loving-kindness for them. For example, the food and drink we consume each day come to us because of the hard work of farmers, lorry drivers, factory workers and shop-keepers. Houses, schools, offices, shopping centres and roads were built by labourers. Many people work to provide us with water, gas, electricity and public services; others produce our clothes and furniture, the books, music and movies we enjoy, and the appliances that make our lives easier. In short, every-thing we have, use and enjoy comes to us from other people.

Other beings are also important from the point of view of our spiritual development. How could we practise ethics — giving up killing, stealing and so forth — without the existence of beings that we *could* kill or steal from? How could we cultivate generosity if there were no one in need? Even enemies are important because they incite our anger and thus give us the chance to work on patience, one of the most valuable qua-lities on the spiritual path. These ideas come from a meditation known as "Remembering the Kindness of Others", which is one of the best methods for developing immeasurable love.

Another factor giving rise to immeasurable love is realizing that all beings are the same in wanting happiness and not wanting suffering. For this there is a meditation known as the "Equality of Self and Others". We think, "Just as I want to stay alive and be happy, so does everyone else. Just as I do not want to experience pain and problems, neither does anyone else." This thought can be used to overcome fear or aversion for people who look strange or who misbehave. It helps us to understand that they are, at heart, just like ourselves.

Furthermore, every being has buddha-nature, the potential to become free and enlightened. Even those who live unethically and do many harmful deeds have a nature that is pure and good, and one day (probably after many lives) they will attain enlightenment. If we can accept these ideas and keep them in mind whenever we meet another living being, then instead of feeling, ''you are different from me,'' we will feel, ''you are just like me'' and loving-kindness will arise naturally.

Love also involves wishing everyone to have the *causes* of happiness. That means we wish them to cultivate positive, wholesome attitudes and behaviour. Giving money, food and kindness fulfils peoples' present needs but doesn't ensure their future happiness. A person may have everything he needs to be happy here and now, but if he does not live ethically and instead acts in a way that harms himself and others, suffering rather than happiness awaits him in the future. Therefore, we also need to help people create the causes of happiness and avoid the causes of suffering.

The love we develop should be pure and unselfish, expecting nothing in return. Pure love is similar to the kind of love a mother feels for her child. When the child is young, the mother is happy to care for all its needs, even though the child cannot give much in return. On the other hand, if we love people as long as they are nice to us but stop loving them when we no longer get what we want, our love is not pure but mixed with attachment and selfishness. This is called ''conditional love'' because it involves demands and expectations. The less self-centred we can be, the more pure and unconditional our love will be.

Pure love also transcends boundaries. It is not right to think ''I love my own children but not other children,'' or ''I love the people in my country but not those in other countries'', or "I am a Buddhist so I love Buddhists but not Christians, Muslims, etc'', or "I'll be nice to humans but not to animals and insects''. To love and help only those of our own race, religion, country or gender is to limit ourselves. If we neglect even one being, our love is not fully developed, not immeasurable.

We might worry that we have enough love for our family and friends but not for every single living being! "If I try to love everyone I'll be exhausted!" But we need not worry about that. Love is an inexhaustible energy. Learning to be more loving is like discovering a natural spring within us: however much love we give, more will always come bubbling up. It is our habitual self-centredness and self-limiting ways of thinking that constrict the flow of love. As we gradually lessen these our ability to love will increase.

We should also be careful to avoid the opposite problem: developing loving-kindness for "all beings" while overlooking the ones around us. It sometimes happens that we have a peaceful meditation on love for all beings, but when we finish meditating we act unkindly to our family members, friends or colleagues! To develop properly, our practice of love should start with the people we live with and meet every day. Gradually we can extend it to beings around the world, in other realms and in distant galaxies!

IMMEASURABLE C*OMPASSION*

*May all sentient beings be free of
suffering and its causes.*

Compassion differs slightly from love. Love wants others to
be happy, while compassion wants them to not have pain,
problems or unhappiness. Love comes from appreciating others'
kindness, or just respecting them as fellow beings, whereas
compassion comes from realizing that they suffer.

Our own experiences of suffering are the basis for compassion. We know what it's like to be sick or in pain, to be
lonely or have our feelings hurt by an unkind remark, to fear
the unknown or mourn the death of a loved one. When we
then see or hear of others experiencing these things, our
heart opens with a feeling of empathy and a wish to help.
This is compassion.

We need to distinguish true compassion from "idiot compassion". We sometimes over-react emotionally at the sight of
suffering. We can be so distressed that we weep uncontrollably,
faint or run away in horror. Our heart may be moved with
pity but our emotions are so out-of-control that we can't do
anything to help! In other cases we might do something but

because we lack right understanding of the problem or the person experiencing it, our "help" only makes the situation worse. These are examples of idiot compassion. True compassion balances loving-concern with clear wisdom. This wisdom enables us to stay calm and think clearly how best to help, without being carried away by our emotions. For example, if someone in our family suddenly becomes ill or has an accident, we need to act swiftly and objectively to relieve that person's suffering and not get caught up by our own fears, anxiety and distress.

When it comes to helping someone who is suffering mentally, even greater wisdom and skill are required. Let's say a friend comes over to see us, upset because his girlfriend has just rejected him. With compassion we listen to his outpour of grief and anger, sympathize with what he's going through and offer kind words to console him. But it would not be right to think that we must solve his problem for him, or to become as depressed and angry as he is. Instead, we should use our wisdom and skilful means to help him come to terms with his problem. For example, we can explain to him that it's not helpful to be angry and revengeful, but that these attitudes will only increase his suffering. He can try to work things out with his girlfriend, but if it looks like the break is irreparable, it's best for him to accept what has happened, forgive and forget, and get on with his life. Throughout our talk together we should try to remain calm, show our concern by listening attentively, avoid preaching or giving unwanted advice, and think clearly how best to help him work out his own solution to the problem. If we can balance compassion with wisdom in this way, he will feel better and we will be able to walk away without carrying his problem on our shoulders.

It is easier for compassion to arise towards some than towards others, but this is only because we have a limited idea of how beings suffer. For example, it is natural for compassion to arise when we see a beggar or a disabled person, but when we see a well-dressed lady driving a Mercedes, we are more likely to feel envy than compassion. That is because we don't realize that she also has suffering. Physically, she has a body that experiences hunger, thirst, heat, cold and tiredness; that gets sick, ages and will one day die. Mentally, she probably has more suffering than a poor person. She must worry about how to maintain her money, position and glamorous image. She may also have problems with her husband or boyfriend, with parents or other family members. She may have a bad-tempered boss, uncooperative employees and jealous rivals trying to harm her. Is it wise to envy such a person?

Moreover, this lady, like all the rest of us, is trapped in the cycle of death and rebirth. Compassion wishes all beings to be free not only from suffering but from its causes as well: karma and disturbing attitudes that keep us in this cycle, or *samsara*. If we want to envy anyone, why not the buddhas and arhats, who are free of death and rebirth, free of all suffering and its causes? Everyone else — even the wealthiest people, even the beings in the highest heavenly realms — has problems and therefore deserves our compassion.

Compassion stops us from harming others. When we see a cockroach in our kitchen, our first impulse might be to squash it out of existence. But stop and think, "This is a living being, who, because of unfortunate karma, has been born in the body of a cockroach, living in dirty places, eating garbage, trying to avoid being stepped on or doused with bug-spray. It wants to stay alive as much as I do. In fact, I could be like that in my next life!" With this understanding, we're more likely to let it live. (If we don't want it to live in our kitchen, we can catch it in a container and take it outside.)

How can we have compassion towards someone who harms us or our loved ones? Compassion involves understanding the situation of others. It asks us to put ourselves in the other person's shoes. "What is he thinking? How does he feel? What makes him behave like this?" If we do this with an open heart, we'll realize that the other person is not happy, that he is not in control of his own mind but rather that he is under the control of his own delusions, which only cause him suffering. This will help us to understand that it is more appropriate to respond with calm patience than with anger and the wish to retaliate.

Being compassionate doesn't mean we have to be passive, weak and say ''yes'' every time we are asked to give or do something. It's alright to say ''no'' if we feel that the request is unreasonable, if we feel we are incapable of fulfilling it, or if the person is simply trying to use us for her own selfish ends. It's also OK to speak up or take action against harm done to ourselves or others, provided we do so with compassion, not anger and aggression.

If we think that an attitude of compassion and non-retaliation is a sign of weakness, some of the great spiritual figures of the past have shown us by their own example that this is not so. For example, Shakyamuni Buddha overcame the negative forces that tried to disturb him on the eve of his enlightenment with the power of his loving-kindness. Jesus Christ compassionately forgave the men who tortured and killed him. Mahatma Gandhi and his followers won India's independence through non-violent activities, even at the risk of death or imprisonment. In this way, they showed us that meeting harm and injustice with compassionate non-violence is far more noble and courageous than fighting back.

IMMEASURABLE

J*OY*

*May all sentient beings
not be separated from sorrowless bliss.*

Immeasurable joy is wishing all beings to have pure happiness, not only in this life but in the future as well. We wish that as long as they are in cyclic existence, they may take rebirth in fortunate states as humans, or devas (celestial beings) or in pure realms. Beyond that, we wish them to attain the sublime peace and happiness of liberation, never again to suffer death and rebirth. To be able to attain that, they must follow the path to liberation, which consists of ethics, concentration and wisdom. Therefore, we wish all beings to learn, understand and practise the Dharma, the path.

Joy also means taking delight in others' success, good qualities and positive actions. For example, we share in the happiness of friends or family members when they pass exams, win contests, get promoted or bring a child into the world; and we admire those who work hard to help others in the community or to advance their spiritual practice. This attitude is known as ''rejoicing'' and it is the best antidote to jealousy.

Jealousy is a very painful feeling that makes us tense and

closed to others. We cannot be happy when we're jealous. Rejoicing, on the other hand, is a beautiful feeling of sharing in others' joy and success. It brings us closer to others. Jealousy is self-defeating. It makes us miserable while others celebrate, and it can lead us to behave in a childish way that attracts criticism rather than the respect we seek.

How do we overcome jealousy? We can reason with ourselves like this: "Whatever happens is due to causes and conditions. If so-and-so did better than I in an exam or competition, it could be because she was more prepared, better disciplined. Or it could be that she has more natural ability, which is due to karma from previous lives. She must have previously created the causes for her success."

It is karma that accounts for differences in intelligence, attractiveness, health, talent and personality. If we are lacking in certain qualities, it is because we failed to cultivate those qualities in previous lives. Being jealous won't change anything. However, if we can accept ourselves as we are with our faults and limitations and then get on with the work of self-improvement, things *will* change for the better.

Rejoicing actually helps bring about this change. To appreciate others' positive qualities and deeds is to encourage ourselves to be like them. When we feel, "How wonderful if I could do what he's doing", we are mentally steering ourselves in that direction. Furthermore, rejoicing is a positive attitude that plants positive seeds in the mind, and that's just what we need to gain qualities and success in the future.

IMMEASURABLE
EQUANIMITY

May all beings abide in equanimity,
free of bias, attachment and anger.

Equanimity is an attitude that involves having equal respect and concern for every being regardless of where they stand in relation to us. In this prayer, we wish all beings to develop the state of equanimity. Practically speaking, however, we must start by developing it ourselves. This involves gradually overcoming the three attitudes that run counter to it: possessive-attachment, uncaring indifference, and anger and ill will.

One of the best ways to overcome possessive-attachment to loved ones is to reflect on impermanence. Everything changes, nothing lasts. One day death will separate us from the people we love. Separation could occur even before that if one of us is posted overseas or if we quarrel and come to hate each other. The more attached we are the more pain and stress we will suffer at this separation. Therefore it is wise to give up attachment. But that doesn't mean giving up love! We can love people without being attached to them by living with the awareness of our inevitable separation. We can appreciate

* * * *

Develop the quiet, even state of mind,
  When praised by some, condemned
by others,
  Free the mind from hate and pride
And gently go your way in peace.

The Buddha

* * * *

and care for them now and at the same time be ready to say goodbye to them when the time comes.

To overcome uncaring indifference towards strangers, those who are neither friends nor enemies, we can reflect on the same meditations that are used to develop immeasurable love, such as thinking about the kindness of others (see page 8). We can think, ''Without others, I would have no food, clothes, shelter or public services. Without others, I could not develop ethics, generosity, patience and the other positive qualities necessary for spiritual growth. Without others, my life would be empty and meaningless.''

It is also good to reflect that a stranger may not always be a stranger. When a person we don't know comes to our aid or rescues us from danger, he or she becomes a lifelong friend.

To overcome anger and ill will towards enemies (an enemy is somebody who hurts us or whom we don't like), we can reflect on the possible causes and conditions of the harm they give us. ''Have I done anything to provoke him? Could it be some flaw in my personality he doesn't like? Perhaps I harmed him in a previous life and he's simply repaying that harm? Maybe his mind is under the control of delusions and he can't help but act this way. That happens to me too, so I should understand what it's like. He must be suffering a lot and he'll suffer more in the future from the negative karma he's creating.'' Thinking this way, we can generate compassion and patient acceptance towards enemies.

Another way to develop equanimity is to remind ourselves that our present relationships will not last forever. From one life to the next, a friend can become an enemy, an enemy can become a friend, a stranger can go either way. Even in this present life our relationships can turn 180 degrees! This happens because our minds are possessed by self-centred attachment, anger and indifference rather than equanimity. Realizing this encourages us to generate the strong wish for ourselves and all beings to abide in equanimity.

Conclusion

This is a brief explanation of how to awaken a kind heart by using the four immeasurable thoughts: love, compassion, joy and equanimity. Each of these four verses is short and can be easily memorized and recited from time to time during the day to remind ourselves to have positive thoughts for the people we meet.

One last word of advice: Don't forget to have loving-kindness for yourself. You are also a living being who deserves, who *needs* love and compassion. In fact, you can't really love others until you learn to love yourself. That doesn't mean being selfish and egotistical. It means being a friend to yourself, accepting yourself as you are with your faults and limitations, knowing that you can change and grow.

It is no use hating ourselves because we are not the way we would like to be, or beating our heads against the wall every time we make a mistake. Doing this only adds more problems to what is already there, and does not help us to improve. But having a kind heart towards ourselves lightens the pain of failures and faults, provides the space in which we can grow, and lays a good basis for loving relationships with others.

TRAINING THE MIND IN COMPASSION

An Explanation of
The Eight Verses of Thought Transformation
by Langri Tangpa

1

With the thought of attaining enlightenment
For the welfare of all beings,
Who are more precious than a wish-fulfilling jewel,
I will constantly practise holding them dear.

2

Whenever I am with others
I will practise seeing myself as the lowest of all,
And from the very depth of my heart
I will respectfully hold others as supreme.

3

In all actions I will examine my mind
And the moment a disturbing attitude arises,
Endangering myself and others,
I will firmly confront and avert it.

4

Whenever I meet a person of bad nature
Who is overwhelmed by negative energy and
     intense suffering,
I will hold such a rare one dear,
As if I had found a precious treasure.

5

When others, out of jealousy,
Mistreat me with abuse, slander and so on,
I will practise accepting defeat
And offer the victory to them.

6

When someone I have benefited
And in whom I have placed great trust
Hurts me very badly,
I will practise seeing that person as my supreme
    teacher.

7

In short, I will offer directly and indirectly
Every benefit and happiness to all beings,
    my mothers.
I will practise in secret taking upon myself
All their harmful actions and sufferings.

8

Without these practices being defiled by the stains
    of the eight worldly concerns,
By perceiving all phenomena as illusory,
I will practise without grasping to release all beings
From the bondage of the disturbing unsubdued
    mind and karma.

INTRODUCTION:

THE PRACTICE
OF TAKING AND GIVING

When you think of the Buddha, his life and deeds, what comes to your mind? Which among his many qualities do you find most inspiring and worthy of respect? I posed this question recently to a group of Polytechnic students whom I have been teaching in Singapore, and nearly every one of them answered, "Compassion." They were inspired by the way the Buddha treated everyone with gentle, kind-hearted compassion; even his rivals and detractors; even his cousin Devadatta who was fiercely jealous of the Buddha and tried on several occasions to kill him. Moreover, the Buddha's compassion extended beyond the human realm to include animals and all other beings, and he taught his followers to practise likewise. The first and most important precept in Buddhism is to try as much as possible to refrain from killing or harming any living being, even the tiniest of insects.

Compassion is a quality desperately needed in the world today. If there could be more compassion in people's hearts and lives, if more people could develop the awareness that: "Just as I do not like being hurt, others also do not like being hurt, so we should stop hurting each other," then there would be far fewer stories in the news about war, terrorism and violent crimes. All the cruel things human beings do to one another are due to a lack of compassion. It is compassion that keeps us from harming others. My teacher, Lama Zopa Rinpoche, has pointed out that if we can develop compassion for all beings, then all beings are safe from being harmed by us. All beings, especially those around us, have nothing to fear from us, so indirectly our development of compassion brings peace to everyone. Imagine what the world would be like if we were all to develop such compassion!

So now the question is, *how* do we develop and practise compassion? Actually, compassion is something that already exists in each and every one of us. It is just a matter of learning how to get in touch with it and how to expand it so that we can feel it more often and for more people. There are many Buddhist texts teaching methods for cultivating compassion. The one explained here, the *Eight Verses of Thought Transformation*, was written by a Tibetan meditator and teacher, Geshe Langri Tangpa, nearly one thousand years ago. It is part of a tradition known as "thought transformation" or *lojong* in Tibetan, which was first transmitted in Tibet by the great Indian master Atisha. His Holiness the Dalai Lama explains thought transformation in the following way:

> The essential message of the *lojong* teaching is that if we want to see a better world, we should begin by improving our own mind. . . . We can spend our life trying to 'tame' the world, a task that would never end; or we can take the more practical path of 'taming' our own minds. The latter is by far the more effective approach, and brings the most immediate, stable and lasting solution. It contributes to our own inner happiness, and also contributes to establishing an atmosphere of peace and harmony in the world around us.[3]

Each of the eight verses of this thought-transformation text

highlights a different way in which we can transform our
thoughts from being uncompassionate and self-centred, to
being more compassionate and concerned about others. This is
because the main obstacle to developing compassion is self-
centredness, also called "the self-cherishing attitude". It is
the self-cherishing attitude that makes us think: "*me* first; my
needs and wishes are more important than those of others."
Cherishing ourselves more than others, we behave uncom-
passionately. For example, there may be an elderly woman
who lives alone in your neighborhood. You are aware that she
is lonely, has few visitors and finds it difficult to get around
or do things for herself because of poor health. You may think
about visiting her and offering your help, but you never actually get around to doing that because you think: "Oh, if I
spend time talking with her or doing things for her, I'll have
less time to do the things *I* want to do." Sounds familiar?
If so, it is not surprising, because the self-cherishing attitude
is something that each of us has.

We *can* overcome selfishness and become more caring and
compassionate. It is just a question of gradually training our
mind, learning to transform our thoughts so that we are less
concerned with *me* — what *I* want, what *I* need, what makes
me happy — and more concerned about *others* — what *they*
want and need, what makes *them* happy. The *Eight Verses*
explains how to do this.

There are several ways of using this text. You could simply
read through it from time to time, pausing to reflect on the
meaning of each verse and how it could apply to your life.
Better still, you could memorize it, so that the verses become
part of your mindstream. This way, when you find yourself in
a difficult situation, the verses may suddenly come to mind,
as if giving you advice on how to handle the situation.

There is also a way of using the *Eight Verses* as part of
a daily meditation practice. To do this, think of, or visualize,

the Buddha or Avalokitesvara (Kuan Yin) in front of you, and read or recite the verses while praying for blessings and inspiration to be able to put the meaning of each verse into practice in your daily life.[4]

The practice of thought transformation, and of compassion itself, is truly challenging. Initially we may feel incapable of practising the *Eight Verses*. But do not be discouraged! Merely reading through them can give us inspiration, and if we are willing to invest time and energy in the practice of training our mind, we will definitely experience a transformation.

Because we all share an identical need for love, it is possible to feel that anyone we meet, in whatever circumstances, is a brother or sister. No matter how different the dress and behavior, there is no significant division between us and others ... our basic natures are the same.

His Holiness the Dalai Lama

VERSE ONE:

THE PRECIOUSNESS OF ALL LIVING BEINGS

With the thought of attaining enlightenment
For the welfare of all beings,
Who are more precious than a wish-fulfilling jewel,
I will constantly practise holding them dear.

The meaning of this verse is: "I, the meditator, wishing to attain enlightenment for the benefit of all sentient beings, will develop the attitude of holding others precious, like a wish-fulfilling jewel."

A wish-fulfilling jewel is a mythical gem that is said to grant all wishes. You hold it in your hands, and when you make a wish like: "I wish I had a Mercedes-Benz," that object suddenly appears out of space. Of course, if such a jewel existed, it would be wonderful to possess it. But this verse is saying that other sentient beings — which means not just other people but also animals, insects and all living creatures — are *more* precious than a wish-fulfilling jewel. This is because a wish-fulfilling jewel can only provide material things — a car, a mansion, a million dollars, and so on. It cannot bring you real happiness or peace of mind. Real happiness — which includes the ordinary happiness we experience in our everyday lives,

29

as well as higher, spiritual forms of happiness such as nirvana
and enlightenment — is the result of creating merit, or good
karma, and in order to create merit, we need others. Let us
see how this works. . .

All the happiness, the good things, we experience in our
life — being healthy, having money and the other things we
need, having kind parents and friends, a good job, and so
on — are the result of merit, or good karma, we created in
past lifetimes. The Buddha said:

> Mind is the forerunner of all actions.
> All deeds are led by mind, created by mind.
> If one speaks or acts with a pure mind,
> happiness follows, as surely as one's shadow.

What does it mean to act with a pure mind? It means acting
with compassion, not harming others and doing only what
helps others. It means being honest and truthful and sincere
in our dealings with others. Without the existence of other
beings as the objects or recipients of our good actions, we
would not be able to create the merit or good karma we need
to experience happiness now. So it is because in past lives
we acted with a pure mind towards others — we refrained
from harming them and instead helped them — that we now
enjoy happiness. So one way in which other sentient beings
are precious is that they enable us to create the merit we need
to experience happiness in our present and future lives.

Another way sentient beings are precious to us is that they
provide us with our needs. We are completely dependent on
others for everything in our lives. Our body comes from our
parents, who also give us the love and care we need to grow,
and who are our first teachers. Our friends fulfill our need
for companionship and intimacy. Other people grow, package
and sell the food we eat each day. All the knowledge and
skills we have were taught to us by others. Everything we
own, use and enjoy comes from others: our house, furniture,

electricity, clothes, books, music, sports facilities, transporta-
tion — everything. Imagine what your life would be like without
the existence of other people!

But the main reason other beings are precious is that
without them we would not be able to attain enlightenment.
Enlightenment, or Buddhahood, is a state of mind free of all
negative attitudes such as anger, greed and ignorance, and full
of positive qualities such as universal love and compassion,
patience, generosity and wisdom. It is the highest, most perfect
state imaginable. Being a Buddha means never having to experience even a moment of suffering — a Buddha is free forever
of all problems and suffering and experiences continuously
the greatest happiness and peace of mind. However, the purpose of attaining enlightenment is not to just sit back and
enjoy this happiness and peace, but rather to be able to help
others become free of their suffering and to lead them to
attain enlightenment as well. That is the real goal — helping
others — and attaining enlightenment is the means to actualize
that goal. So the correct motivation for wanting to attain
enlightenment is the compassionate wish to benefit others.

To achieve this wonderful happiness of a Buddha, we need
to develop positive states of mind, such as loving-kindness,
compassion, generosity and patience. And to develop these
qualities, we need other people, other living beings. We cannot
develop loving-kindness, the wish for others to experience
happiness, if there is no other being to love. Nor can we develop compassion, the wish for others to be free of suffering,
without becoming aware of the suffering of others. Similarly,
how could we practise generosity, which involves giving to
others what they need — food, money, medicine, protection,
comfort, spiritual guidance and so on — if there were no beings
in need of these things? And with whom could we practise
patience if we never met anyone who stirred up our anger?

This is why we cannot attain enlightenment without other
sentient beings. In fact, we cannot attain any of the stages

or realizations of the spiritual path without them. So other sentient beings are extremely precious, far more precious than a Mercedes-Benz, a million dollars, or a wish-fulfilling jewel. When we realize how precious others are, we practise "holding them dear", which means respecting them, cherishing them, caring for them, avoiding giving them any kind of harm and doing what we can to help them.

VERSE TWO:

DEVELOPING HUMILITY AND RESPECT

Whenever I am with others
I will practise seeing myself as the lowest of all,
And from the very depth of my heart
I will respectfully hold others as supreme.

In the first verse, we start to view others as precious and important. Here, in the second verse, we go a step farther and try to see them as *more* important than ourselves. The text says: "When I am with others, I will always try to see myself as the lowest of all and, with great respect and heartfelt sincerity, I will hold others as supreme."

Seeing ourselves as the lowest of all does not mean putting ourselves down, or hating ourselves, thinking, "Oh, I'm terrible. I'm hopeless. I'm worthless. I'm the worst person in the world." That is not what is being expressed here at all. What it means is that we need to overcome pride.

Pride and self-importance cause us to look down on others and even to disregard or mistreat them. This is a hindrance to our spiritual development. If we are to grow spiritually, we need to cultivate an attitude of respect for others, to cherish them and keep our mind open to learning from them. Pride is one of the greatest obstacles to this. Because of pride, we may even feel superior to spiritual teachers and to those who sincerely wish to help us, and so reject the advice or help they have to give.

It is pride that makes us mentally compare ourselves to other people we know or meet. When we find that we are in some way better, this fuels our feelings of self-importance: "I'm more intelligent than him . . . I'm more attractive than her. . . I'm better educated . . . I'm more talented." When we feel superior to others, we tend to be more critical and judgmental of them. Quietly, in our mind, we make lists of other people's faults and mistakes, and look down on them — as if we had no faults of our own!

On the other hand, if we find that the person to whom we are comparing ourselves is in some way superior, we feel jealous and resentful. These feelings of jealousy and resentment are also related to pride; they arise as a result of our own wish to be superior. All these attitudes are unhealthy; they disturb our mind and obstruct our spiritual development. They also prevent us from having positive and satisfying relationships with others. How can we really love and care about others, when we cannot even respect them?

There is a story from the life of Milarepa, an esteemed Tibetan Buddhist saint, that illustrates the disadvantages of pride. Three attractive young women, all dressed up in their finest clothes, were walking along a road when they came upon a poor, thin, bedraggled-looking man sleeping by the roadside. They were shocked by his appearance and one of them exclaimed: "Oh, I pray that I shall never become like *that*!" The man was Milarepa, and his poor appearance was the result of long years spent meditating in caves, living on little more than nettles. He was actually a Buddha — through his strong practice of meditation he had attained the state of enlightenment and his mind was completely pure — but he did not look so fantastic on the outside! Milarepa was not really asleep and when he heard the young woman's comment, he opened his eyes and said to her: "You couldn't be like me even if you wanted to!" When the young women realized who he was, they felt ashamed, begged his forgiveness and requested him to teach them the Dharma.

Since pride is not helpful and brings only problems, we need to put effort into developing its antidotes of humility and respect for others. One way of doing this is to train ourselves to see the good qualities of others, rather than their faults. That is what this verse is all about. It is not telling us to put ourselves down, but rather to stop putting others down and ourselves up. Instead of focusing on our own qualities and on other people's faults and mistakes, we should direct our attention to our own faults and focus on the good qualities of others. It is very easy to see faults in others and to criticize them, but once we realize that this does no good at all, and in fact only causes problems, we can train ourselves to do the opposite. We can always find something good in others, even in the worst person in the world. So try to always look for good qualities in others and to remember the positive things they have done. The great Indian master Atisha said: "Look for your own faults, do not look for those of others. Hide your own good qualities, do not hide those of others." I think this is very good advice.

If we take this verse to heart and practise it, we will become more humble, more respectful towards others and less critical. As a result, our mind will be more happy, less negative, and our relationships with others will improve.

VERSE THREE:

CULTIVATING MINDFULNESS

*In all actions I will examine my mind
And the moment a disturbing attitude arises,
Endangering myself and others,
I will firmly confront and avert it.*

This verse is about the practice of mindfulness. Mindfulness means watching the mind, being aware of what is going on inside: "What am I thinking? What am I feeling? What is happening in my mind?" When we are mindful, it is easier to see disturbing attitudes arise, and to take action to prevent them from harming ourselves and others.

What are disturbing attitudes? They are the negative thoughts or emotions that arise in our mind. We experience both positive and negative attitudes. Positive attitudes such as kindness, caring, patience and generosity make our mind peaceful and our behavior refined and considerate towards others. Negative attitudes include anger, jealousy, pride, greed and selfishness. When these attitudes arise they disturb the mind, making it agitated and unpeaceful. They also lead to unskillful and harmful actions, like hitting or beating someone, or verbally criticizing a person with harsh, unkind words that hurt their feelings. Not only do these actions harm others, they also leave imprints on our mind that will ripen in the future in some form of difficulty and unpleasant experience, such as sickness, failure, poverty, loss, being abused and so forth. In fact, all of the sufferings we and others experience in our lives are the result of the previous negative actions we committed under the influence of disturbing attitudes.

Furthermore, allowing our mind and our behavior to be influenced by disturbing attitudes creates obstacles to our spiritual development. In our future lives, we will not be able to encounter spiritual teachings and spiritual teachers who can guide us on the path to liberation and enlightenment. Instead, we will find ourselves in difficult circumstances and amongst people who nurture our negative qualities, thus we will fall deeper and deeper into confusion and suffering. These are some of the reasons why this verse says that disturbing attitudes ''endanger'' oneself and others.

In order to protect ourselves and others from the harmful effects of disturbing attitudes, we need to guard ourselves with mindfulness, recognize disturbing attitudes when they arise and do something about them before they become strong enough to influence our behavior.

There are several ways we can ''confront and avert'' our disturbing attitudes. One is to apply an antidote, something opposite to that particular disturbing emotion, such as meditating on compassion as an antidote to anger,[5] or on joy as an antidote to jealousy.[6] Another way is simply to let it go. Disturbing emotions are not permanent, fixed aspects of our personality. They are just temporary mental states that come and go in the mind. They arise when the right causes and conditions have come together, exist for a short time, and then disappear. If we take them too seriously, and identify with them — for instance, having the feeling ''*I* am angry'' — then we attribute to them undue strength and validity, and that makes it easier for them to take control of us. So, instead of

thinking: "I am angry," try thinking: "Anger is in my mind."
Remind yourself that it is just an experience, a mental state
that comes and goes in the mind, and see if you can let it go.
Let it go out of your mind, like a cloud drifting away, or like
a bubble that bursts and disappears. Just let go of it. Do not
let it stay and disturb your mind.

Of course, there will be times when neither of these methods
will work. For example, sometimes our anger is so strong that
we just cannot let go of it or replace it with compassion or
love. It takes hold of our mind and we simply cannot forget it.
In this case it is good to think about the faults of anger, its
disadvantages. Generally, anger makes our mind unhappy
and unpeaceful. It prevents us from enjoying food and other
pleasures. When our mind is full of anger we cannot rest during
the day or sleep well at night. It also clouds our mind so that
we cannot think clearly or make wise decisions. Instead, we
tend to speak or act in irrational, uncontrolled ways that upset
or even frighten other people and afterwards we feel ashamed
and regretful. Even if we apologize and are forgiven, some
damage has been done. Anger, therefore, is like a mental
illness, or a poison, which harms both ourselves and others.
Reminding ourselves of the drawbacks of anger and the other
disturbing emotions can help us to generate the wish to avoid
them and instead turn our mind to more positive attitudes.

There will also be situations when delusions arise very
abruptly and we have no opportunity to work on them. For example, we may get angry at work when we are criticized by our
boss or a colleague, but have no chance to sit and meditate on
the faults of anger, or on its antidotes of love and patience. In
such a situation, we should try to keep the anger from spilling
over into our speech or behavior — that is, try to avoid saying
or doing anything out of anger, since that would just bring
more problems. We may need to do something to keep calm,
like taking a few deep breaths, counting to ten, saying a prayer
or mantra, or leaving the room until we have cooled down.

But these are merely short-term ways of dealing with anger, to avoid losing control and doing something we would later regret. They enable us temporarily to suppress the anger, but not to get to the root and really deal with it. So what we need to do, when we have cooled down a bit and have some time and space, is to sit down, think back over what happened, and try to understand why we got angry. By using clear, rational thinking, we may then be able to recognize mistakes we made — for example, being too quick to take offence, having unreasonable expectations of the other person, not really understanding the other person's point of view, or just not having enough patience! Learning from our mistakes, we can think over how we might do better next time, if we were to find ourselves in a similar situation in the future. We might even be able to transform our attitude towards the person with whom we got angry by replacing anger with a more positive attitude such as acceptance or compassion.

In conclusion, we need to recognize the disadvantages of disturbing attitudes such as anger — how they are harmful to ourselves and to others — so that we will try harder to avoid being taken over by them. When they do arise, we can practise either letting go of them, or cultivating their positive counterparts. The important thing is to not act on the disturbing thoughts when they arise since this just leads to problems both now and in the future.

Where there is suffering, there is peace and
bliss, by letting go and experiencing it
for numberless suffering sentient beings.
Always think of how others are kind and
precious. Treat them as you would like to be
treated. With this practice, the beautiful
lotus heart blossoms and the happiness sun
shines delightfully in your life.

Lama Zopa Rinpoche

VERSE FOUR:

CHERISHING
THOSE WHO ARE DIFFICULT

Whenever I meet a person of bad nature
Who is overwhelmed by negative energy and intense
  suffering,
I will hold such a rare one dear,
As if I had found a precious treasure.

Can you recall ever having met or seen the kind of person described in this verse? It may have been someone you suspected of being involved in criminal activities, gambling or prostitution. Or perhaps it was someone who appeared to be dishonest, bad-tempered, arrogant, greedy, lustful or extremely selfish. How did you feel towards this person? Uncomfortable? Frightened? Annoyed? Repulsed? Judgmental? Did you try to avoid that person and to keep your distance?

Similar feelings can arise when we see people who appear to be very poor, who are homeless, mentally ill, or behaving in a disturbing way. Although this kind of reaction is quite understandable, this verse is advising us to regard such people as especially dear, like a precious treasure.

Why is this? Well, it is natural to be attracted to people who are kind, friendly or good-looking. It is easy to associate

41

with people like that. But when it comes to difficult people, those who are very angry, demanding, irritating, cruel or even frightening, in such cases our positive, loving feelings are really put to the test. We have an opportunity to see that our patience and kindness have definite limits, and that we need to put more effort into expanding these qualities.

Difficult people do not pose a problem for Buddhas and bodhisattvas. Spiritually mature beings like these never feel fear or aversion towards anyone; they only experience love and compassion equally for all living beings. We too can learn how to keep our hearts open to even the most difficult people, by working on changing our attitudes and perceptions. One way to do this is to remind ourselves constantly when we are with others: "This person wants to be happy just as I do, and just like me does not want to experience any problems or suffering. The reason he or she is behaving in a disturbing way is because of strong delusions and negative imprints in the mind. This outer behavior and appearance is a reflection of the inner delusions and imprints obscuring the mind. But these are temporary, not permanent. Like everyone else, this person's real nature is pure and good and has the potential to attain enlightenment. One day he or she will be free from the delusions that are causing so many problems right now, and will attain the state of enlightenment."

One of my teachers, Kyongla Rato Rinpoche, said that it is important to separate a person from his or her delusions, and to attribute a person's bad behavior to the delusions, not the person. For example, if we read in the newspaper about a man who has just been convicted of murder, instead of blaming the person and thus feeling angry and judgmental, we should understand that it was the delusions in his mind — ignorance, greed, hatred, or whatever — that motivated him to commit the crime. That way, it is easier to be tolerant and kind-hearted towards the person, and feel the compassionate wish for him to be free from his suffering and delusions.

It is also helpful to reflect that this person probably has *more* suffering than other people, and so is in greater need of kindness and compassion. There is an account of a Tibetan Lama who visited one of the former Nazi concentration camps in Germany which had been converted into a museum. Gazing at a picture of soldiers torturing a prisoner, he commented: "I feel more compassion for the torturers than for the victim." When asked why, he replied: "Because the suffering of the victim is over fairly quickly, but the suffering of the torturers will last a very long time." You see, when people become caught up in delusions such as hatred, cruelty or obsessive greed, their minds are deeply disturbed, not at all peaceful and joyful, and through their behavior they create even more problems and suffering for themselves in the future.

Thinking in these ways can help us to overcome feelings of fear and anger. We may even feel motivated to extend a helping hand to those who are troubled and needy. However, we also need to use our wisdom. Sometimes it may not be within our capacity to benefit others who are very negative-minded, and trying to do so can even bring us harm. In such cases, it may be best to keep a distance from such people, while keeping a compassionate and open-hearted attitude towards them. We should remain calm and peaceful in their presence, as this may have a beneficial effect on them. Also, we can pray for them, and pray that we may be able to help them more in the future when the time is right. Such thoughts and prayers create the cause for our mind to become more like the minds of the Buddhas and bodhisattvas, so that in the future we will become capable of helping even the most difficult people.

Because difficult people provide us with the opportunity to recognize that our patience and love have limits, and that we still have shortcomings like aversion and selfishness that need to be overcome, they are very beneficial for our spiritual development. Realizing this, we will be able to hold them dear and cherish them, like "a precious treasure".

VERSE FOUR:

OFFERING
THE VICTORY TO OTHERS

When others, out of jealousy,
Mistreat me with abuse, slander and so on,
I will practise accepting defeat
And offer the victory to them.

This verse suggests a skillful way of responding when somebody insults us, criticizes us, or spreads rumors behind our back. They may do this out of jealousy, or simply because they do not like us. Our usual reaction in such cases is to feel hurt and angry. We may become defensive and immediately retaliate, or we may remain silent, bottling up our anger. Although such reactions are normal, they are not so skillful. When we get angry, whether we express it or keep it inside, our mind is disturbed and unable to think clearly and rationally. Anger never helps, it only brings problems like resentment and conflict, and plants the seeds for future suffering. As an alternative to anger and retaliation, this verse advises us to patiently accept the situation and to let the other person have the victory.

How can we develop this kind of attitude? Well, one thing we can do is to check our mind, to question why we respond the way we do. Why do we feel hurt and angry when someone says bad things about us? Why are we so concerned about what other people think and say about us? Does the opinion of others make us what we are? If other people dislike and criticize us, does that necessarily mean we are bad? Alternatively, if others like and respect us, does that necessarily mean we are good?

Giving too much credence to what others say about us can cause us to be emotionally unstable and to have an unrealistic view of ourselves. When criticized, we feel devastated and depressed, and can lose our self-confidence. When praised, we feel elated and puffed up with pride, and may come to think we have no faults. There is a story from the Tibetan tradition about a man who was liked and respected by everyone in his community, and as a result of that came to feel that he was quite a wonderful person. But just before he died, he realized with dismay that all the respect and praise he had received had made him blind to his faults, so that he had neglected to work on himself, on his spiritual development. So instead of basing our self-image on what others think and say, it would be wiser to look honestly and objectively at ourselves. Only we can know the truth about ourselves, what we are really like inside: our positive qualities and the areas of ourselves that need to be worked on. With a realistic view of ourselves, we will not be so affected by others' opinion.

But this does not mean that we should completely ignore what others say, because criticism can be useful. One of my teachers, Geshe Doga, once said that there is never any reason for us to get upset if we are criticized. We should look inside ourselves and check whether the criticism is true or not. If it is not true, then the other person's words are like empty, meaningless noise, and there is no need to get upset about them. But if we check and find that the criticism is true, then we can gratefully accept it as helpful advice for our spiritual development. It is often difficult to see ourselves objectively — we tend to be blind to our faults and mistakes, so when others point them out it can be useful for us.

Another reason why we may get upset when we are criticized is that we want to always be right, to always be the
winner in any argument or conflict. So it may be useful to ask
ourselves: "Why is winning so important to me? And what does
it mean to 'win'?" If we fight and win an argument in such
a way that the other person is left feeling humiliated or bitter,
will we really feel good about ourselves? Have we achieved
something that we are satisfied with? And are things really
so black and white that there is necessarily a winner and
a loser in every conflict? Could it be that "winning" and
"losing" are relative, that they are just ideas or concepts in
our mind, depending on how we interpret a situation, depending on what we want and expect from the situation? In other
words, if we have a clear idea in our mind as to what we really
want to achieve, it may be possible to settle a problem between
ourselves and another person in such a way that we both come
away feeling the better for it.

Another method is to reflect on karma. If we check our response to the criticism, we may notice our mind saying things
like: "This isn't fair. I haven't done anything to deserve this.
This shouldn't be happening to me!" Think again. According to
karma, or the law of cause and effect, whatever difficulties
we experience now are the result of our previously-committed
negative actions. These actions may have been committed in
another life or in the present life — we can probably recall
instances in this life where we spoke negatively about others.
Now we are reaping the results of those actions. So we can
say to ourselves: "There is a reason why this is happening
to me. In the past I must have harmed others by insulting
them and spreading rumors. Now, I am experiencing the same
situation in return. If I get angry and retaliate, that will create
more negative karma and as a result, I will have to experience
even more problems in the future. So the best thing I can do
is to accept what is happening patiently."

We might also try to cultivate compassion for the person

who is criticizing us. It is quite likely that she is in a very disturbed state of mind, and not at all peaceful or contented. If so, we can generate compassion by thinking: ''She is saying these harmful things because of the anger and jealousy in her mind. Anger and jealousy are very unpleasant and disturbing, so it is impossible to be peaceful and happy while such emotions are in the mind. Also, she is not really in control of what she is doing; she is controlled by her delusions. As a result, she is suffering now, and will also suffer in the future when she has to experience the karmic results of her present actions.'' If we can look at the situation in this way, it will be easier to feel compassion and not wish to give harm.

All this does not mean that we should never defend ourselves when wrongly accused or blamed. For example, there may be cases where it is appropriate for us to stand up for ourselves, speak the truth and clear false accusations or rumors. However, we should try to do so without anger, without the wish to take revenge.

Nor does it mean that we should not attempt to communicate with someone who is angry with us. If the person is open to communication and we are able to speak calmly and without anger, it may be possible to work out a solution to the problem that we are both happy with. What is being stressed in this verse is that we should avoid acting or speaking out of anger, bitterness and so forth, or harboring such thoughts in our mind towards those who harm us.

In most cases of being criticized, our response arises from our attachment to reputation — wanting others to like and respect us. According to the Tibetan masters, this is one of the most difficult attachments to let go of. There is a story from the Tibetan tradition about the Kadampa Geshe Langri Tangpa, author of the *Eight Verses*, that illustrates how a spiritually mature person is free from such concerns. Once, a woman who had given birth to a sickly child was told by an astrologer that in order to save the child's life, she must take it to a spiritual master and claim it was his. So she brought the child to Langri Tangpa, who happened to be in the middle of giving a Dharma discourse to a large number of disciples, and put it on his lap saying: "This is yours." The Geshe happily accepted the infant and said: "For all my lives you have been my child." Seeing this, half of the disciples lost faith in their teacher and walked out. But Langri Tangpa continued to teach. At the end of the discourse, the mother presented the Geshe with offerings and apologized to him for what she had done, explaining that she had been advised to do it in order to save the child's life. Langri Tangpa calmly handed back the child. He had maintained equanimity throughout this whole incident, and the half of the disciples who had not walked out experienced even greater faith in their master.

Langri Tangpa was able to remain calm in this situation because he knew that he was innocent of any wrong-doing, and because he was not attached to what others thought of him. He was not concerned about being the "victor". If we are willing to look honestly at our mind and work on diminishing our attachment to reputation and praise, then we will also learn to remain calm in the face of criticism and blame.

VERSE SIX:

Learning
FROM THOSE WHO HARM US

When someone I have benefited
And in whom I have placed great trust
Hurts me very badly,
I will practise seeing that person as my
supreme teacher.

The situation described here is more difficult to deal with than those in the previous verses, because here, the person who harms us is someone we are close to — it could be a friend, a family member, or a student — someone we have helped, and who we expect to treat us with consideration and kindness. Instead, this person betrays our trust and hurts us. The pain we experience in such a situation is far greater than that experienced when we are hurt by someone with whom we are not so close. And this hurt and pain will most likely make us feel angry and bitter. We may even think of how we could harm the person in return. However, this verse advises us to practise seeing that person as a "supreme teacher". What does that mean? How can we come to see this person as our teacher?

First of all, we can examine the feelings of love and caring

that we had for the person. Was our love pure and unconditional, asking nothing in return? Or was it conditional, tied up
with expectations? Most of the time, we place expectations on
our friends and loved ones. In exchange for the love, friendship,
care and help that we give to them, we expect them to be
nice to us, to do what we want them to do, and not to do what
we do not want them to. In this way, our relationships are
somewhat like business contracts, with a whole set of unwritten
rules: "I will do this for you, provided you do that for me;
I will be nice to you as long as you are nice to me; I will help
you as long as you do what I want." This kind of love is called
"conditional love" — love with strings attached. It is not real
love. Real love is unconditional. It is a sincere, heartfelt caring
about the other person, with respect and acceptance of them
just as they are, without demanding or expecting anything
in return.

It is dangerous to have expectations of other people, because
they do not always live up to our expectations; they do not
always act the way we want them to. In some cases this may
be deliberate — they may truly intend to hurt us — but in
most cases, they are simply being themselves, doing what they
want to do. If this happens to go against what we want them
to do, then we feel hurt, disappointed and even angry.

So the real problem is not so much what the other person
did or did not do, but rather that we had expectations of them
that they did not fulfill. So we need to check if our expectations
were reasonable and realistic. We can ask ourselves: "What
exactly were my expectations? Was I being realistic and fair?
Or was I expecting too much? Would it be right for me to stop
caring about this person simply because he didn't live up to
my expectations?"

This brings us to the reason why this person is such a
valuable teacher. He has given us the opportunity to recognize
the limits of our love. We discover that our love was not free
from conditions, and was not strong enough to withstand hurt

and betrayal. We may then decide that we need to work harder at developing pure, unconditional love. Therefore, if we find ourselves in the kind of situation described here, where we have been hurt by someone we trusted and our mind is filled with painful, disturbing thoughts and emotions, it is useful to regard the situation as a valuable lesson, and to regard the harm-giver as a teacher. He has given us the opportunity to understand ourselves better, to see our limitations and to become aware of the areas we need to work on to perfect our love. In fact, that person is a *supreme* teacher, because it is only through facing difficulties such as this, that we can develop real love, compassion and wisdom, and progress along the spiritual path.

You may argue: "But his intention was not to teach me or help me — his intention was to hurt me." It is not necessary for people or things to *intend* to help us in order for us to receive help from them. The sun, for example, has no intention of helping us but everyone in the world benefits from its light and warmth. It is all a matter of how we choose to look at things. If we learn something important from a person or an experience, even a painful one, then it becomes helpful for us, even if there was no such intention involved.

Difficult situations also give us an opportunity to learn about and work on developing our patience. Patience is a valuable asset, because it enables us to remain peaceful and joyful, no matter what happens. We all have a certain amount of patience, but it is limited, and when somebody pushes us beyond our limits, we become angry. So we need to keep extending the boundaries of our patience, and a person who harms and upsets us provides us with the perfect opportunity to do this. Difficult situations are a valuable test. If we never go through this kind of test, we can fool ourselves into thinking: "I'm a very patient person. Nothing can disturb me." But such thinking hinders our spiritual growth. Getting angry makes us realize we are not as patient as we like to think! Then we can humbly say to ourselves: ''Now I can see that I still have a lot of anger, and I need to work more on developing patience.''

So that is why a person who hurts and betrays us is like a teacher. He or she teaches us that we still have a long way to go in order to perfect our love and patience, and also gives us the opportunity to put both of these qualities into practice.

VERSE SEVEN:

THE PRACTICE
OF TAKING AND GIVING

In short, I will offer directly and indirectly
Every benefit and happiness to all beings,
*   my mothers.*
I will practise in secret taking upon myself
All their harmful actions and sufferings.

This verse describes a practice called "taking and giving", or *tong-len* in Tibetan. This is a very powerful meditation technique used by those who are following the bodhisattvas' path to strengthen their love and compassion and to awaken the mind of enlightenment. It involves imagining that one is *taking* on the suffering of others, and *giving* to them one's own happiness and virtue.

How does this practice work? Well, the main obstacle to developing love, compassion and the mind of enlightenment is the self-cherishing attitude. This is the habitual tendency that we all have to think primarily of our own welfare, happiness, needs and wishes, and to neglect the happiness and well-being of others. It is the thought: "I want happiness and don't want to suffer, but I don't care about the happiness and suffering of others." This attitude needs to be reversed

53

if we are to reach enlightenment, and the practice of taking and giving is a very effective way gradually to overcome self-cherishing and to develop its opposite: the mind that cherishes others.

When we do this practice of "taking and giving", the "taking" usually comes first. This is because it is difficult for people to be truly happy while they are experiencing suffering. Someone who is very ill, for example, would find it hard to enjoy the things that normally give him pleasure until he regains his health. Therefore we need to first remove others' sufferings, and then give them happiness. We begin by meditating on the various sufferings that other people are undergoing, such as sickness and pain, aging and dying, failure, dissatisfaction, fear, grief and so on, and generate a strong, compassionate wish that all beings be free of these sufferings. We then go a step further and feel the wish to actually take their suffering upon ourselves. With this compassionate thought, we visualize all the sufferings in the form of black smoke and imagine drawing the smoke into our heart. At our heart, we visualize our self-cherishing attitude in the form of a black stone or spot. When the black smoke of others' suffering is drawn into this black spot at our heart, the spot becomes smaller and smaller until it finally disappears. At that point we feel joyful, thinking that now all beings have been freed from their suffering, and our own self-cherishing attitude has been overcome.

Initially, it may be difficult to sincerely wish to take on all the sufferings of others. We may feel: "I can't even handle my own problems, so how can I take on those of others?" Because of this, it is often advised to start the practice of "taking and giving" by taking on our own present and future suffering. The procedure is the same as above, but instead of focusing on the sufferings of other beings, we focus on whatever problems and difficulties we are now facing in our life.

We visualize taking all these problems into our heart and imagine that doing so diminishes and destroys our selfishness. Then we think of those we can expect to face in the future — such as sickness, loss, conflict with others, frustration and disappointment, growing old and eventually dying — and visualize in the same way. Once we feel comfortable about accepting and transforming our own suffering, we can move on to imagine taking on the suffering of people with whom we are close, such as parents, relatives and friends. Eventually we will be able to take on the suffering of strangers and even of those whom we dislike.

There is a simple way of practising "taking" that can be used whenever we experience a problem — whether it be physical pain or sickness, or an emotional problem such as loneliness, fear, hurt, grief and so on. Normally we feel aversion to any kind of problem or unpleasant experience, and wish it to disappear as quickly as possible. We may also get caught up in self-pity, and feel as though we're the only person in the world who is suffering. This is just adding more problems to what is already there, and creates a lot of tension in our mind. Instead of this, we can use the problem to open our heart and cultivate compassion. Start by thinking: "I'm not the only one who has such a problem. There are many other people, many other beings, who are experiencing the same problem — in some cases far worse than mine." Reflect on that for some time — see if you can think of specific examples. . . . Then think: "How wonderful it would be if all those other people and beings could be free from this suffering." Really *feel* that compassionate wish. . . . Next, decide to accept your own problem on behalf of all those other beings: "I accept this problem, this suffering, and by my accepting it, may all those other beings be relieved of theirs." This method works like magic — it brings peace and spaciousness to our mind, lightens our suffering, and expands our compassion for others.

It is by having compassion and the thought
of universal responsibility that one finds
the happiness of life, the real joy of life,
the real meaning of life: one feels real peace
and happiness in one's heart.

Lama Zopa Rinpoche

If we find it hard to understand the wish to take on others' suffering, we can think of how parents feel when they see their children in pain. Parents have so much love and concern for their children that they cannot bear to see them suffer. They may even feel: "I wish I could take away my child's suffering. I would rather experience it myself than have my child suffer!" When a mother or father has this kind of love they would willingly sacrifice their own well-being in order to take on their child's suffering and give it their happiness in exchange. This shows that where there is strong love and compassion, people are able to generate the kind of selfless attitude expressed in this verse. In fact, we all have this potential. We can all develop universal love and compassion, and we can all develop the sincere wish to take on the suffering of others and to give them our happiness. It is just a question of training the mind.

After we have visualized freeing all beings from their sufferings by taking those sufferings onto ourselves and thereby destroying our self-cherishing attitude, we turn to "giving". For our practice of "giving" to be powerful we need first to meditate on loving-kindness, the wish for all beings to have happiness and the causes of happiness. We meditate on loving-kindness until we feel this so strongly that we wish to give our own happiness to others. The actual meditation on giving involves visualizing all the good things we have — our happiness, good qualities, wisdom and accumulation of virtue — in the form of light. We then imagine sending this light out to others and when it reaches them, it transforms into whatever they need in order to be happy: food for those who are hungry, money for those who are poor, medicine for those who are sick, friends for those who are lonely, and so forth. Since everyone needs Dharma in order to attain the highest, most perfect happiness of enlightenment, we also imagine the light transforming into Dharma teachings and visualize that by receiving these, the beings attain all the realizations of the path up to enlightenment. Then we meditate on a feeling of great joy, thinking that all beings are now fully satisfied and perfectly happy.

You may wonder why the verse says: "all beings, my *mothers*". This refers to the idea that each and every living being has been our mother — not in this present lifetime, of course, but in our previous lifetimes, which are said to be countless and without beginning. In fact, we have been in every possible type of relationship with every living being, but that of mother and child is emphasized because, generally, our mother is more important and more kind to us than anyone else. She brings us into the world, feeds us, nurtures us with love and affection, protects us from harm, teaches us basic skills like walking and talking, and so on. Once we realize the vast kindness of our mother, and think of all beings as having been mother to us, we will feel closer to them, and will want to repay their kindness by helping them as much as we can.

When we are more familiar with the practice of taking and giving, we can combine it with our breathing: as we breathe in we imagine taking in others' suffering, and when we breathe out we send out our happiness to others. This is an advanced level of practice, and a way to create immense merit and get closer to enlightenment with every breath!

You may wonder: "By doing this practice, will I actually receive someone else's sickness? And can I actually give happiness to someone who is unhappy?" The answer is that it is very unlikely. According to the law of cause and effect, or karma, each of us is responsible for our own actions, and thus our own suffering and happiness. No one can take away another person's negative karma and suffering, or give them one's own good karma and happiness. If it were possible to do so, the Buddha would have removed all our suffering and given us the perfect peace of enlightenment long ago! "Taking and giving" is practised to train our own mind: to develop compassion and loving-kindness, and to overcome the self-cherishing attitude. By developing our mind in this way, eventually we will achieve enlightenment and will then possess unlimited resources with which to help and guide others to freedom from suffering, karma and delusions. Nonetheless, by practising taking and giving with sincere compassion and love, we may be able to provide some relief to those who are suffering, and help them to feel more calm and peaceful.

VERSE EIGHT:

THE ILLUSORY NATURE OF PHENOMENA

*Without these practices being defiled by the stains
    of the eight worldly concerns,
By perceiving all phenomena as illusory,
I will practise without grasping to release all beings
From the bondage of the disturbing unsubdued
    mind and karma.*

There are two very important Buddhist teachings contained in this verse. The first is the need to keep our Dharma practice pure, free of the eight worldly concerns. The second is the understanding of the real nature of all phenomena — that they are like an illusion. Understanding the illusory nature of all phenomena will free us from disturbing emotions and karma, and then we can help others likewise to become free.

What are the eight worldly concerns? They are concern about gain and loss, pleasant and unpleasant experiences, praise and blame, and the wish to have a good reputation and not to have a bad one. When we have these eight attitudes, we feel happy when we receive or possess things, unhappy when we lose or are unable to get what we desire; happy when we have pleasant experiences, unhappy when we experience pain or anything unpleasant; happy when someone praises us, unhappy when we are blamed or criticized; happy when our reputation is good, unhappy when our reputation is bad or we are unknown.

All these eight concerns can be condensed into two attitudes: being attached to what is pleasant and having aversion or fear towards whatever is unpleasant. In other words, whenever we encounter or obtain something pleasant our mind feels happy and excited and becomes attached to whatever brought us that pleasure, be it a person, an object or an experience. On the other hand, whenever we encounter someone or something unpleasant, ugly, frightening or uncomfortable our mind feels unhappy, irritated or angry and develops aversion towards that object.

One of the best examples of this is our reaction to praise and criticism. When people point out our good qualities, or tell us that we have done something really well, we feel happy. Our mind goes up and we feel elated and excited. But whenever we face the opposite — criticism, blame or unkind words — what happens? Our mind goes down and we feel depressed, unhappy and negative. We may even become angry and want to hurt the person who criticized us.

Gain and loss is another major concern. When people give us gifts, when we go shopping and buy something nice for ourselves, or when we get something we want like a raise in salary, we feel happy and excited and get attached to the object or to the person who gave it. But when we do not get what we want, or when we lose something that we cherish, our mind goes down and we become unhappy, depressed and angry.

This is what the eight worldly concerns are all about: being overly concerned about the good and bad things that happen in our life. What is wrong with that? Well, if we allow our mind to be influenced by these eight attitudes then they leave us at the mercy of conditions over which we have no control, such as what people think and say about us, or whether we encounter good or bad experiences. As a result of that, our mind and our mood is always up and down like a yo-yo on a string — one moment happy, the next moment unhappy; one moment full of love and kindness, the next full of anger and resentment. These eight attitudes cause our mind to be uptight and fearful; we are afraid of losing the things we are attached to and of meeting what we do not like. These eight attitudes also tend to be self-centred — they are concerned about getting what *I* want, and avoiding what *I* do not like — and thus are an obstacle to developing genuine concern for others. They get us all caught up in experiences and things which are impermanent, and which we will have to leave behind when we journey to the next life. Furthermore, under their influence, we may act unwisely, such as behaving pretentiously in order to win others' attention and praise, or stealing things we desire but cannot afford to buy. The eight worldly concerns are thus a source of problems in this life and an obstacle to our spiritual development.

This is not to say that it is wrong to experience pleasure and to not want. There is nothing wrong with pleasant experiences, relationships, a good reputation, money or material possessions. The problem is being *attached* to these things. Attachment is a mental state that tends to exaggerate the positive qualities of people and objects, overlooks their shortcomings, gets lost in fantasies about them, and desires never to separate from them. It is therefore unrealistic in outlook, and leads to problems such as possessiveness, feeling disappointed when things don't turn out the way we imagined they would, and falling into depression when we lose the things we're attached to. What we want is happiness, but attachment is actually an obstacle to that. It makes our mind disturbed and tense, such that we are unable to just relax and enjoy people and experiences. So the problem is not the pleasant experiences themselves, it's our attachment to them.

We need to be especially alert to the eight worldly concerns influencing our practice of Dharma. For example, we may want people to be impressed by our Dharma knowledge, by our patience or our diligence in observing precepts, by the amount of money we donate to a charitable cause or the amount of time we spend doing social work. We hope that others will notice how long we are able to sit in meditation with our back perfectly straight, looking serene and sublime like the Buddha. We are full of enthusiasm when our practice is going well, but when we encounter problems we become depressed and discouraged, and think about giving it up. These are signs that the eight worldly concerns have crept into our Dharma practice. When this happens, it means that our practice has become polluted or ''defiled'', and is actually the cause of further confusion and suffering rather than of peace, happiness and spiritual growth.

So what should we do if we notice any of these eight attitudes in our mind? First, we should not be upset with ourselves, thinking: ''Oh, I'm such a bad person to feel this way!'' Instead we should be happy that we have become aware of a problem that we have always had but never noticed before. Now we can do something about it: we can change our mind and develop more positive, realistic attitudes.

The best remedy to the eight worldly concerns is to reflect on impermanence: the changing nature of all things. The pleasant and unpleasant events and experiences of this life are not permanent — they last only a short time and then disappear. So it is unwise to cling to what is pleasant, wishing it to last forever, or to be upset by what is unpleasant, since it will soon vanish. Furthermore, our very life is impermanent: we are going to die one day and when we do, everything in this life — relationships, possessions, pleasant and unpleasant memories, reputation, and so on — will fade and disappear like last night's dream.

A Dharma practitioner learns to think like this: ''My life

is going to end at some point. I am going to die and leave everything behind: loved ones, possessions, job, reputation, all my experiences, even my body. Only my mind will go on to face the next life. In order to ensure that my mind can remain peaceful and positive at the time of death, have a smooth transition to the next life, and obtain a fortunate rebirth, I must learn to overcome disturbing negative states of mind such as attachment and aversion. I need to practise Dharma purely, without the pollution of the eight worldly concerns.''

The second teaching contained in this verse is that all phenomena are like an illusion. This refers to the Buddha's teaching on emptiness, also known as ''selflessness''. Emptiness is the actual, correct way in which everything exists: oneself, all other people and living beings, all inanimate phenomena. It is the ultimate, true nature of all things. Emptiness is not somewhere far away or up in space; we do not have to travel to a place like the Himalayan mountains to find it. Emptiness is right here, right now: it is the true nature of our bodies and mind, our thoughts and feelings, and everyone and everything around us.

Emptiness is not nothingness; it does not mean that things do not exist at all. Things *do* exist, but they do not exist the way we think they do. Our mind projects a way of existing onto the objects we perceive — like an extra layer on top of what is actually there — and then we believe that things really do exist that way. However, they are *empty* of the false, mistaken way of existing that our mind projects onto them. That false way of existing is called ''inherent existence'', ''independent existence'' or ''true existence''. It means that we see things as if they were permanent, independent, existing from their own side, in and of themselves. If we carefully analyze, we will come to see that things do not exist in this way — that such a way of existing is false, an illusion.

Take a flower, for example. When we walk into a room and

see a flower in a vase, we instinctively perceive the flower as something permanent, unchanging, existing all on its own, as if it did not depend on anything else for its existence. It seems very real, concrete, out there, existing in and of itself — almost as if it is saying: "I'm a flower. I've always been here and always will be here, just like this!" This is how the flower appears to us and we believe it to exist in this way. But this way of appearing and the actual way the flower exists are quite different. In reality the flower is impermanent, dependent on various causes and conditions, and not existing in and of itself. The flower came into existence in dependence upon a seed, soil, moisture and sunlight. It grew little by little and when it was in full bloom, someone cut it and placed it in a vase. Its existence is also dependent on its parts: stem, petals, leaves, as well as on the cells and atoms that make it up. When first cut, the flower was fresh and beautiful but as the days go by, it withers and turns brown, and soon it will die and be thrown away. That is the true story of the flower, but that is not what we see when we look at it. When we look at it, it seems to be permanent, unchanging and independent of anything else.

Furthermore, our mind grasps at the object being a flower from its own side, not realizing that "flower" is just a name people have given to a certain phenomenon with certain characteristics, and that people of other languages would call it by other names. So, although there appears to be a real, solid, permanent and independently-existing flower existing out there, in and of itself, when we investigate and search for such a flower, it cannot be found. Such a flower is an illusion — like a dream or a rainbow. It appears, but does not exist the way it appears. But this does not mean that there is no flower at all. There *is* a flower — an impermanent collection of parts that came into existence in dependence on causes and conditions, is changing and will go out of existence, and to which we give the name "flower". *That* exists, but not the permanent, independently-existing flower that we perceive and grasp at when we say: "Oh, isn't it beautiful!"

In the same way, all things appear to be permanently, inherently, independently existent, but on closer examination, we realize that they exist in a completely different way. And that is their reality, their true nature: being empty of inherent existence.

"So what?" you may wonder. "Why should I be concerned about this?" We should be concerned because this tendency to perceive, believe in and grasp at things as truly existing or inherently existing lies at the root of all our problems. Fear, worry, frustration, dissatisfaction, loneliness, grief, pain, and all the other myriad problems and sufferings of mind and body that we experience are caused by this attitude, which in Buddhism is known as "self-grasping ignorance". We all have the potential to enjoy ever-lasting peace, bliss, wisdom and freedom from all suffering — the state of enlightenment or Buddhahood — but we are unable to attain this as long as our mind is caught up in ignorance, and does not understand the true nature of things.

Self-grasping ignorance pervades our view of everything. We see ourselves as inherently existing — we cling tightly to an illusory image of a permanent, independently existing I or self. We hold on to self-limiting concepts about ourselves, believing that mistakes made in the past have become permanent aspects of our personality. These "permanent faults" become the basis of low self-esteem and even self-hatred, obscuring our potential to be pure, perfect and free — an enlightened being. All this arises from ignorant misperception.

Moreover, we tend to cherish our sense of self, as if it were the centre of the universe. Out of this strong self-centredness, we develop desire and attachment for people and things that make us happy and support our sense of I, we have aversion and fear towards people and things that disturb us or threaten our sense of I, and we are indifferent towards whoever or whatever neither helps nor harms us. Believing all these people and objects to also exist in a real, permanent, independent way further intensifies our attitudes of attachment and aversion. These attitudes disturb our mind and motivate us to create negative actions or karma, such as harming our enemies, and lying or stealing to benefit ourselves and our loved ones, and this karma is the cause of suffering and problems in the future. Self-grasping ignorance is also the main factor that keeps us circling in samsara, the cycle of death and rebirth.

That is why we should be concerned about our tendency to see things as truly or inherently existent, and why we should learn to perceive things in their correct way, as empty of inherent existence, or, as it says in the verse, as "illusory". Perhaps a simple way to understand this is by thinking of the analogy of a rainbow. Due to certain conditions in the atmosphere and the play of sunlight and moisture, a rainbow appears in the sky. Although it looks so real we would like to touch it, it is insubstantial, momentary and completely dependent on causes and conditions. It exists for a while and then disappears. Everything else, all conditioned phenomena — animate and inanimate — can be compared to a rainbow. Although most things last longer than a rainbow, the way they exist is similar: they arise due to the coming together of different causes and conditions, exist for a while, and then, again due to causes and conditions, they go out of existence. So, like a rainbow, they are illusory, empty of permanent, independent, substantial existence.

Keeping in mind that all things are illusory, a bodhisattva engages in the practice of Dharma, the path leading to enlightenment, without grasping at anyone or anything as truly existing. In this way the bodhisattva frees him- or herself from disturbing states of mind and karma — the causes of all suffering in the prison of samsara — and works to help all other living beings to likewise become free.

For a long as space endures
    And for as long as living beings
    remain,
Until then may I too abide
    To dispel the misery of the world.

                                        Shantideva

CONCLUSION

My intention in this explanation of the *Eight Verses* has been to show the relevance of this precious little text, from another time and another culture, to our lives in this present time. In my own experience I have found these verses to be extremely helpful. They teach us different ways of looking at and dealing with difficult situations, so that in place of feeling disturbed and unhappy, we can remain calm, clear and compassionate. Practising them takes courage and strength, but if we are able to do so, we will grow tremendously in wisdom and unselfishness. I am certain that, deep down in our hearts, that is what we all long for.

It is said in the prayer-ceremony, *The Guru Puja*:

> In brief, the childish labor only for their own end,
> While Buddhas work solely for the welfare of others.
> With a mind understanding the distinctions between
>   the failings of one and the advantages of the other,
> We seek your blessings to enable us
> To equalize and exchange ourselves for others.[7]

"Equalizing and exchanging ourselves for others" involves

making the decision to change our attitude and our focus, from being self-centred and self-cherishing, to cherishing others. We come to this decision by understanding that all beings are equal in wanting to be happy and to not experience any suffering, and on top of this, understanding that self-cherishing brings only problems while cherishing others is the source of all happiness and goodness.

The Buddha attained the perfect peace of enlightenment long ago, but our minds are still confused and disturbed, and we are helplessly trapped in the cycle of birth, death and suffering. The main reason for this is that the Buddha gave up his self-cherishing attitude long ago, whereas we are still very much attached to ours. We too can achieve what the Buddha achieved, but we must work on ourselves. That means putting effort into changing our mind, our attitudes: being less self-centred, more concerned for others; less angry, more patient; less grasping, more detached; less unkind, more compassionate.

We *can* change, provided we are willing to train in practices like those explained in the thought transformation teachings. But, remember, it takes time to change the mind. It is not something that we can expect to happen in a few months or even in a few years. Therefore, we need to be patient and compassionate towards ourselves. What that means is to compassionately accept ourselves as we are now, while knowing that it's possible to change the way we are, and to steadily put our energy into practices that will enable the changes to take place.

Notes

1. *The Dalai Lama, A Policy of Kindness.* Compiled and edited by Sidney Piburn. (Ithaca, New York: Snow Lion Publications, 1990), p. 52.
2. For more information on this text, its background and author, see Geshe Tsultrim Gyeltsen, *Keys to Enlightenment* (Los Angeles: Thubten Dhargyey Ling Publications, 1989), pp. 47-50.
3. Gyalwa Gendun Druppa, the First Dalai Lama, *Training the Mind in the Great Way.* Translated by Glenn H. Mullin (Ithaca, New York: Snow Lion Publications, 1993), p. 12.
4. A practice composed by Lama Zopa Rinpoche, which combines visualization and prayer to Avalokitesvara with meditation on the Eight Verses, can be found in *Pearl of Wisdom, Book II*, published by Amitabha Buddhist Centre, Singapore, 1991. For a short commentary to the practice, see Kathleen McDonald, *How to Meditate* (Boston: Wisdom Publications, 1984), pp. 160-170.
5. For an explanation of how to develop compassion, see pp. 11-14.
6. For an explanation of how to develop joy (rejoicing) as an antidote to jealousy, see pp. 15-16.
7. *The Guru Puja* (Dharamsala: Library of Tibetan Works and Archives, 1979), p. 43.

GLOSSARY

The words in italics are Sanskrit.

Arhat — one who has attained nirvana, or complete liberation from suffering, but has not yet attained enlightenment.

Atisha (982–1054) — a great Indian master and scholar who came to Tibet to help in the revival of Buddhism and established the Kadam tradition. His text *Lamp on the Path to Enlightenment* became the first in a tradition of teachings called the graduated path to enlightenment (*lam rim* in Tibetan).

bodhicitta — the aspiration to attain full enlightenment in order to help all beings.

bodhisattva — a being who has developed bodhicitta and is striving for enlightenment for the sake of all beings.

Buddha — a fully-enlightened being; one who has overcome all obstacles and completed all good qualities and is therefore able to benefit all other beings to the maximum extent.

Buddhahood — see enlightenment.

compassion — empathy with the suffering of others; the wish that other beings be free from their suffering.

delusion — a mental state that causes our mind to be disturbed, and leads us to deal with people and situations in mistaken, harmful ways, thus resulting in problems. Examples are: anger, jealousy and attachment.

Dharma — spiritual teachings and practices; any knowledge or method that frees us from confusion and suffering; specifically, the Buddha's teachings.

emptiness — the actual way in which all things exist; the absence of the apparent independent existence of things.

enlightenment — the highest, most perfect state of mind, in which all negative aspects of mind have been eliminated, and all positive qualities have been perfected; Buddhahood.

equanimity — an even-minded attitude towards everyone, cultivated by overcoming the habit to classify others as either friend, enemy or stranger.

ignorance — not understanding truth, especially the ignorance that fails to understand emptiness, the actual way all things exist.

impermanence — the ever-changing nature of all things that arise from causes and conditions.

inherent existence — the falsely-conceived mode of existence of things, in which things seem to exist from their own side, independent of anything else.

joy/rejoicing — the attitude of appreciating and feeling happy about positive, virtuous actions, both one's own and others'; taking delight in others' good qualities, success, good fortune, and so on.

karma — the law of cause and effect; the process whereby

virtuous actions lead to happiness and non-virtuous ones to suffering.

liberation — the state of complete personal freedom from suffering and its causes, delusions and karma.

love — the wish that other beings have happiness and its causes.

mantra — a series of syllables, usually Sanskrit, that are recited as part of one's spiritual practice. Mantras can be recited for various purposes, e.g. purification of negative karma, or development of compassion or single-pointed concentration.

meditation — the process of becoming familiar with positive states of mind, through both analytical investigation and single-pointed concentration.

merit — positive energy created when one performs virtuous actions.

mindfulness — awareness, especially awareness of one's own thoughts, feelings, attitudes and behavior.

nirvana — see liberation.

samsara — the cycle of death and rebirth, fraught with suffering and dissatisfaction, that arises due to the ignorance of the true nature of all things.

sentient being — a being who has consciousness, and has not yet attained enlightenment.

thought transformation — teachings and meditation methods for the purpose of training one's mind in the attitudes and practices of a bodhisattva, e.g. compassion, love, patience, inner strength, wisdom, etc.

wisdom — the correct understanding of things, especially the correct understanding of emptiness, the ultimate, true nature of all phenomena; the main antidote to ignorance.

SUGGESTED FURTHER READING

Chodron, Pema. *Start Where You Are.* Boston: Shambhala Publications, 1994.

Chodron, Thubten. *Open Heart, Clear Mind.* Ithaca, New York: Snow Lion Publications, 1991.

Dilgo Khyentse Rinpoche. *Enlightened Courage.* Ithaca, New York: Snow Lion Publications, 1994.

Essence of Refined Gold: Selected Works of the Dalai Lama III. Compiled, edited and translated by Glenn H. Mullin. Ithaca, New York: Snow Lion Publications, 1982.

Gyalwa Gendun Druppa, the First Dalai Lama. *Training the Mind in the Great Way.* Translated by Glenn H. Mullin. Ithaca, New York: Snow Lion Publications, 1993.

Gyeltsen, Geshe Tsultrim. *Keys to Enlightenment.* Los Angeles: Thubten Dhargyey Ling Publications, 1989.

Kongtrul, Jamgon. *The Great Path of Awakening.* Translated by Ken McLeod. Boston: Shambhala Publications, 1987.

McDonald, Kathleen. *How to Meditate.* Edited by Robina Courtin. Boston: Wisdom Publications, 1984.

Rabten, Geshe and Geshe Ngawang Dhargyey. *Advice from a Spiritual Friend*. Boston: Wisdom Publications, 1984.

Shantideva. *A Guide to the Bodhisattva's Way of Life*. Translated by Stephen Batchelor. Dharamsala: Library of Tibetan Works and Archives, 1981.

Wallace, Alan B. *A Passage from Solitude: Training the Mind in a Life Embracing the World*. Ithaca, New York: Snow Lion Publications, 1992.

Wangchen, Geshe Namgyal. *Awakening the Mind of Enlightenment: Meditations on the Buddhist Path*. Boston: Wisdom Publications, 1987.

Yeshe, Lama Thubten and Zopa Rinpoche. *Wisdom Energy*. Boston: Wisdom Publications, 1987.

Zopa Rinpoche, Lama. *Transforming Problems into Happiness*. Edited by Ailsa Cameron and Robina Courtin. Boston: Wisdom Publications, 1993.

ACKNOWLEDGEMENTS

The publication of *Awakening a Kind Heart* was made possible because of the generosity of the following persons:

Mr Koh Thong Joo and Ms Liem Siu Tju, who made a donation towards this project to commemorate the occasion of their marriage; and also

Mr Benny Law.

If you have enjoyed reading this book,
please share it with a friend.
Or you may like to make a contribution towards
keeping it in print by sending a donation to
Amitabha Buddhist Centre, c/o Publications Subcommittee.

THE AUTHOR

Venerable Sangye Khadro, an American nun, was ordained in 1974. She has taught Buddhism and meditation at centres around the world and is currently resident teacher at Amitabha Buddhist Centre, Singapore, a position she has held for the past seven years. She is the author of *How to Meditate*.

AMITABHA BUDDHIST CENTRE

Amitabha Buddhist Centre is a centre for the study and practice of Mahayana Buddhism from the Tibetan Vajrayana Tradition. Our aim is to provide a friendly and conducive environment for people to contact, learn and put into practice the teachings of the Buddha. We also seek to serve the wider community through a variety of spiritual, educational and social welfare projects.

ABC is under the guidance of the Venerable Lama Thubten Zopa Rinpoche. We run an active programme of events led by our resident Venerable teachers.

To find out more of our activities, please call us to request a copy of our monthly newsletter or visit us at the address below:

Amitabha Buddhist Centre
494-D Geylang Road
Singapore 389452
Tel: (65) 7458547
Fax: (65) 7410438
E-mail: fpmtsing@singnet.com.sg
Web Page: http://www.singnet.com.sg/~fpmtsing